I0473647

The Small Business Reference Guide

The Complete Guide to Small Business Taxes and Business Startup

Minute Help Guides

Minute Help Press

www.minutehelpguides.com

© 2011

Table of Contents

Introduction

It is estimated that over 1,600 new businesses are started each day. While entrepreneurship has been forced upon many people during the economic downturn, most people who start a business do so in pursuit of a dream, or the quest for independence and financial security. The U.S. government, through its tax code, encourages entrepreneurship and small business start ups by providing small businesses with a number of tax incentives.

For small businesses, it is a double-edge sword, as the tax code can also be frustratingly complicated. The unfortunate reality is that many business owners, already overwhelmed with the demanding tasks of starting and managing their business, fail to treat the tax aspects of their business as a year-round endeavor. As a result, they are unable to take full advantage of the tax incentives, and worse, they fall into traps that can be very costly.

The purpose of this guide is to help you navigate the maze of tax issues that confront small businesses each day in order to make the filing process far less taxing.

How to Use this Guide

While this guide should not be considered a substitute for the detailed information on small business taxation available through IRS publications (see the section on Online and other Resources), nor should it replace the expert guidance of a tax professional, it will help you to streamline the learning process to better utilize those resources should you need them. When it comes to taxes, especially for business owners, your learning curve is shortened significantly when you start out by knowing what it is that you do not know, which is the purpose of this guide.

This guide is constructed on a modular basis to enable you to quickly familiarize yourself with the essential components of business tax planning. Many of the tax issues covered apply equally to all types of businesses, however some are more specific to the various forms of business. The simple format of this guide will enable you to focus only on those issues that apply to your type of business.

Section 1: Small Business Taxation Overview

Section 2: Planning Your Business for Tax Efficiency

Section 3: Record Keeping Essentials

Section 4: Paying Your Estimated Taxes

Section 1: Small Business Taxes Overview

Creating a Legal Tax Entity

As the owner of a small business, you become, in the eyes of the IRS, two distinct tax entities. The purpose of your enterprise is to generate profits which will become your form of income. The IRS wants know about both so it can determine the legitimacy of your business as well as its share of your profits and income. To do that, it has established specific guidelines and requirements for establishing a business as a legitimate tax entity. There are five key steps to getting on board with the IRS:

Obtain an Employer Identification Number (EIN)

Form a legal business structure

Establish a tax timeframe

Establish a business accounting method

File and pay your taxes

If you employ people in your business there are additional requirements that will be discussed in this section as well.

Step 1: Obtain an Employer Indentification Number (EIN)

An EIN establishes your indentity with the IRS, so that when you file your tax returns it will recognize you as a legitimate business. For most businesses an EIN is the recommended form of identification, however some businesses, such as a one-person home-based enterprise could get by with a Social Security number. If you plan on hiring employees, opening a business checking account, establishing a qualified retirement plan, or operating as any form of business other than a sole proprietorship, you will need an EIN.

Your business identification number is used on any document or form that is submitted to the IRS to report any income that you have received in the conduct of your business.

How to Obtain an EIN

The easiest way to obtain an EIN is to go online and apply directly with the IRS at www.irs.gov/businesses/small. The number is issued instantly after your information has been verified. You can also call 1-800-829-4933 between the hours of 7:00 a.m. and 10:00p.m, or submit Form SS-4 through the mail, but this could take more than a month to receive your number.

Step 2: Form a Legal Business Structure

Every small business must be organized as a legal business entity using one of four forms: Sole proprietorship, partnership, or corporation. A limited liability company (LLC), while a legal business form, is not recognized by the IRS as a distinct tax entity. Each form has its advantages and disadvantages, both from a legal standpoint as well as for tax planning. The one you choose will depend on a number of factors, including your particular tax and financial situation, the amount of liability exposure your business has, and the amount of time and money you are willing to expend in the formation of your business.

Sole Proprietorship

Considered to be the easiest business structure to form, it is most suitable for individual business operators who don't anticipate hiring employees or acquiring a lot of business assets. It requires no forms, fees or legalities unless you want to file a DBA with your state. The income of a sole proprietor business flows directly through from the business to the business owner, so taxes are filed on a personal income tax return.

Partnership

In its simplest form, a partnership is a merger of two more sole proprietors, requiring no forms, fees or rules for operation. However, it is recommended that partners enter into a partnership agreement, which is a legal document specifying participation and buy out arrangements. As with sole proprietors, the income of the partnership flows through to the partners, so taxes are filed individually on the partner's personal tax returns.

Corporation

A corporation is the only business form that is recognized as a distinct tax entity. The income, losses, expenses and taxes of a corporation all occur within the structure of the business, which is required to file its own, separate tax return. Forming a corporation involves legal documentation and specific rules of operation and fees. Depending on the type of income that is distributed to the shareholders, it could be subject to double-taxation – taxed first to the business and then to the shareholder.

Sub Chapter S Corporation

S Corps are sort of a hybrid of a corporation and a partnership in which the business operates under the rules and requirements of a corporation. However, the profits, losses, and expenses flow through to the shareholders as in a partnership. This is used instead of a corporation when the objective is to prevent double-taxation. There are very strict qualifications for establishing an S Corp.

Limited Liability Company (LLC)

Although LLCs are a legitimate business structure in the eyes of your state, the IRS does not recognize them as distinct tax entities. LLCs are used to obtain the same level of limited liability that corporations have against debts and legal actions. The business is treated, for tax purposes, more like a partnership with "pass through" taxation.

An overview of tax planning considerations for each form of business is provided in Section 2, Planning Your Business for Tax Efficiency.

Step 3: Establish a Taxable Timeframe

The IRS wants your business to account for income based on a predetermined twelvemonth timeframe, either as a calendar year (January through December) or a fiscal year (any consecutive twelve month timeframe that ends on the last day of any month except December).

Once a taxable timeframe has been established and a tax filing has already occurred, it requires the approval of the IRS to convert to another. This includes instances when a business owner changes the structure of the business from one form to another.

Generally, a calendar year timeframe is used if, in your business, you don't keep separate accounting or you don't meet certain IRS guidelines for using a fiscal year.

Step 4: Establish a Business Accounting Method

The IRS wants each business to follow prescribed rules when accounting for their income and expenses. Your accounting method is determined the first time you file your return and you cannot change it without prior approval from the IRS. The two forms of accounting accepted by the IRS are the cash method, and the accrual method.

Cash Method

This is a simple accounting method in which your business income is reported in the year that it is received. All expenses are applied in the same tax year.

Accrual Method

Instead of reporting income in the tax year in which it is actually received, business income is reported in the year it is earned. Expenses are applied as they occur, not necessarily when they are actually paid. The accrual method is usually used when a business has inventories or requires materials that may be involved in transactions, but where payment has not yet been made.

Step 5: File and Pay Your Taxes

Estimated Taxes

Although you are only required to file one tax return per year, you may be required to file and pay estimated taxes throughout the year. For all business forms except corporations, estimated taxes must be paid if they anticipate owing at least $1,000 in total taxes for the year. Form 1040-ES is used to calculate and pay estimated taxes. Corporations must pay estimated taxes if they expect to pay at least $500. They use Form 1120-W.

Paying the Tax

Most employers are required to actually pay their taxes before they file a return at the end of the year. Employment taxes, excise taxes and estimated taxes are typically paid throughout the year. If the total amount of your tax deposits, including income and Social Security/Medicare withholdings don't exceed a certain threshold, you can make your tax deposits through your business bank using a deposit coupon (Form 8109). Otherwise, these taxes must be paid using the Electronic Federal Tax Payment System (EFTPS). When you apply for your EIN, you will be automatically enrolled in EFTPS which issues you a PIN and instructions for accessing it.

More on Deposit Coupons

When you obtain a new EIN, you will typically receive a deposit coupon from the IRS. When you make a deposit using the coupon, you must include your EIN and tax period on your payment check to ensure proper crediting. Additional coupons can be ordered directly from the IRS.

For more information on Estimated Taxes, see Section 4, Paying Your Estimated Taxes.

Filing Information Returns

Your business may receive and make payments to a number of different payees, and for most of them, the IRS wants an accounting. This is usually done using one of several different types of information returns, which are then compiled by the IRS at the end of the year to compare your information with the payee's information.

The most popular information return used by employers is Form 1099-Misc in which payments of more than $600 made for certain types of services or business needs are reported.

For payments made to employees that are considered compensation of any kind, Form W-2 must be filed. The W-2 is also where any tax withholdings are reported. Both the IRS and employees receive a copy of the W-2.

If your business receives a cash payment of any kind in excess of $10,000, it must be reported on Form 8300.

Hiring Employees

There are specific filing and reporting requirements when hiring new employees.

Employment Eligibility Verification

As part of the hiring process, you must be able to verify that your new employee meets the eligibility requirement for obtaining employment in the United States. To do this, you would have them complete Form I-9, Employment Eligibility Verification.

Social Security Verification

You must obtain verification of your new employees Social Security status. A copy of their number, or better yet a copy of their card, should be made part of their employment record and recorded on Form W-2.

Tax Penalties

For just about every tax and filing requirement outlined above, there is a penalty for non-compliance, including failure to file, pay, report or withhold taxes as required. In most cases, the penalty consists of some percentage of the taxes not paid or reported plus interest, which can be very costly. In almost every instance, the penalties could have been avoided. Here are some of more frequent penalties assessed by the IRS on small businesses:

Inaccurate Reporting

One of the more frequent mistakes small businesses make is inaccurately reporting income or business deductions. If the IRS determines that it was the result of negligence or carelessness, you could be assessed a 20% penalty. These inaccuracies are usually uncovered during an audit. If you are unable to verify an expense or explain underreported income the agent will assess a penalty.

Willful Underreporting of Income

If your underreported income was willful, rather than just negligent, you fine increase to 75% of the unpaid tax. Aside from the penalty, you may be subject to criminal tax fraud.

Failure to Pay on Time

For each month that your taxes remain unpaid, the IRS will tack on a penalty of .5% to 1% of the unpaid tax.

Failure to File on Time

Filing a late tax return will also result in a penalty which is 5% on the unpaid taxes up to 25%.

Underestimating Estimated Taxes

Another frequently assessed penalty is for underestimating the estimate tax. While you don't have to be spot on with your estimate, you need to at least be close. As a general rule, if your earnings are less than $150,000, you need to come within 10%, or just pay an amount equal to your previous year's tax. If your earnings exceed $150,000, you need to have paid at least 110% of your prior year's tax.

Your quarterly estimated payments need to be paid in equal installments. You can still be penalized if you underestimate in your first three installments and then try to catch up in your fourth.

Incorrect or Missing Information Returns

One of the biggest traps small businesses fall into is the failure to file the appropriate information return, such as the 1099-Misc, or Form 8300. Misreported W-2s are also a frequent occurrence, and, if they are not corrected in time, a penalty will be assessed. If missing or corrected forms are filed by August 1 in the year that your returns are due, and if the number of these missteps doesn't exceed 1% of the total number of information returns you file, you can avoid the penalty.

Business Taxes in General

For most small businesses the only tax with which they need to concern themselves is the income tax. As your business grows, depending on its legal structure, additional taxes may be required.

The most common forms of business taxes are:

Income taxes

Self Employment taxes

Employment taxes

Sales taxes

Excise Taxes

Income Taxes

The IRS requires all businesses to file a tax return. If your business is a sole proprietorship, partnership, S Corp or LLC, your business income is reported through the filing of your own personal income tax return. If you are structured as a corporation, a separate tax return is filed for your business.

The income a business report is generally a net figure that includes all business revenue and profits minus expenses and depreciation. The income is reported differently depending on your form of business.

Sole Proprietor: Net business income is calculated on a Schedule C and reported on your 1040

Partnership: Partnerships do not file a tax return. The partners calculate their proportionate share of income and expenses on Schedule E and report net business income on their 1040. The partnership is required to file an information return (Form 1065) and a K-1 schedule of income and expenses to each of the partners.

Corporation and S Corp: Income taxes are filed using Form 1120 (1120S for S Corps). Additionally, for an S Corp, each shareholder must include their share of income, as reported to them from the K-1 schedule on their 1040.

More on the Schedule K-1

For any business that uses a pass-through structure, such a partnership or S Corp, the IRS requires a Schedule K-1, which is a complete breakdown of each partner's or shareholder's proportionate share of profits, income and expenses. The K-1 is similar to a 1099 form received by an employee to be used to complete a tax return.

Self-Employment Tax

One of the tax surprises for new business owners is the self-employment tax which, of course, is only applied to people who are self-employed. The tax is, essentially, your contribution to the Social Security and Medicare systems, and is required to be paid if your income exceeds $400. Schedule SE is used to calculate your tax that is reported on your 1040. The good news is that half of your self-employment tax may be used as an adjustment to your gross income on your 1040.

Employment Taxes

Employment taxes are applied to businesses that have employees and include Social Security and Medicare taxes, Federal income tax withholding, and Federal unemployment tax. Many businesses hire independent contractors, and sometimes make the mistake of not including them in their tax reporting. For purposes of employment taxes, independent contractors may fall within the classification of an employee.

Federal Unemployment Tax (FUTA)

Each employer pays into the unemployment compensation fund on behalf of their employees. The FUTA tax is paid using form 940, Employer's Annual Federal Unemployment Tax Return.

Sales Taxes

If your business is involved in the sale of goods or services, your state may have a requirement that you collect sales taxes. Your business is responsible for collecting sales taxes from your customers and then reporting and paying them to the state.

Excise Taxes

Depending on the type of business you have, you may be required to pay federal excise taxes, which are taxes applied to the sale, manufacture or use of certain kinds of products or equipment. For instance, if your business utilizes heavy trucks on public highways, you may be assessed a tax on its use. Taxes are assessed on a variety of products, materials or business equipment that effect the environment, or are involved in interstate communications or transportation. Businesses that sell or manufacture certain types of heavy equipment or vehicles are also subject to the tax.

The excise is calculated and filed using Form 720, Quarterly Federal Excise Tax Return. Excise taxes owed on the use of heavy vehicles on public highways are filed using Form 2290.

Tax Withholding

Income and Social Security/Medicare taxes must be withheld from an employee's income payment. You would use Form W-4 to determine how much income tax to withhold from each payment. For Social Security and Medicare tax withholding, you can refer to IRS Publication 15 to determine the amount.

Each quarter an employer needs to file Form 941, the Employer's Quarterly Federal Tax Return, which reports the withholdings for income and Social Security/Medicare taxes. Also, the employer's share of each employee's Social Security and Medicare tax is paid with this form. At the end of the year, the employer issues each employee a W-2 form that includes an accounting of all their withholdings during the year.

Business Expenses

Perhaps the biggest advantage in owning a business is the fact that most expenses incurred in the conduct of your business are deductable from your business income, which can have the effect of increasing your net income. Small businesses in their early stages of growth often report negligible taxable income, or even losses, because business expenses are likely to exceed business revenue. The potential danger is that, if your business shows more than a couple of years of losses, the IRS will question its legitimacy. It is important to be able to demonstrate to the IRS that your business has a profit purpose and will be able to generate profits eventually.

Deductibility of Expenses

Business expenses that are considered to be ordinary and necessary in the operation of your business are deductible, which means every expense dollar will lower your reportable income by a dollar. Certain expenses are applied differently depending on the type of business you operate.

Cost of Goods Sold

If your business manufactures products or resells them, expenses incurred in the production or sale of the products will be used to determine the cost of goods, which is what is deducted from your gross revenue. Expenses such as labor costs, inventory management, storage, retail commissions, materials costs, and sales costs are all expenses that go into determining your cost of goods.

Capital Expense

When outlays are used to purchase a business asset or invested in your business for start-up or improvement purposes, it is classified as a capital outlay which, instead of being deducted, would be capitalized to produce deductions over time. In some instances, business start-up investment may be deducted up to $10,000 in the first year of operation.

Personal Expenses

Personal expenses are generally not deductible unless they are incurred for something that has both a business use and a personal use. The best example is in the business use of your home. Generally, expenses such as your mortgage, home insurance, depreciation, maintenance, and utilities can be deducted to the extent that your home is used for business. If 10% of your home's space is dedicated to your business, you may be able to deduct a proportionate part of each expense.

Car expenses can also be split as personal and business expenses, and deductions taken in proportion to its use for business.

Other Business Expenses

Employee compensation: Any form of compensation that is received by employees is a direct business expense. This includes contributions to health plans and retirement plans.

Business rent: If you rent or lease property specifically for your business it is deductible.

Insurance: Most forms of business insurance are deductible. Liability insurance, business property insurance, and surety bonds are forms of deductible insurance expenses.

Interest expense: Interest incurred from any borrowing to finance your business operations is deductible.

Taxes: Taxes incurred by your business, such as local, state, sales, and some federal taxes may be deductible.

Advertising and marketing: If not used to calculate cost of goods sold, these expenses can be applied as direct deductions.

Section 8, Getting the Most from Your Business Deductions, provides additional tips and techniques for maximizing your deductions.

The Small Business Jobs Act – Overview

As part of the economic recovery efforts, Congress passed the Small Business Jobs Act. In recognition that small businesses are the engine of the economy, generating as many as 90% of the nation's jobs, the act was passed to stimulate small business growth. In addition to the provisions that addressed small business lending, the act included several provisions designed to ease their tax burden.

Most of these provisions effect or change some of rules and guidelines outlined in this guide. They are listed separately here, because several of them are only temporary, which means that the rules and guidelines will revert back. Here are some of the key provisions that affect the taxes of many small businesses:

Enhanced Section 179: Section 179, which is covered in Section 8 (Getting the Most from Your Business Deductions), is a method small businesses can use to write off the full value of a capital outlay in the year they are made, as opposed to spreading the recovery out over several years. The change increases the upper limit of the deduction from $250,000 to $2,000,000 for the 2011 tax year.

Elimination of capital gains on small business investments:

Continued 1st year depreciation bonus: Small businesses were granted a temporary acceleration of capital expenditure deductions for years 2008 and 2009, which allowed them to write off 50% of the cost of most new personal property. The act extended the bonus depreciation for another year.

Increased Start-up business deduction: Allows a new business to deduct up to $10,000 (up from $5000) for start-up expenditures.

Increased exclusion of gain from sale of stock: Increased from 75% to 100% the amount of gain that may be excluded from the sale of qualified small business stock that is held for at least five years. The stock must have been purchased after September 2010.

Five-year carry back for credits: Small businesses with less than $50 million in average gross revenue can carry back unused business credits for five years instead of one to offset taxes paid in prior years.

Business credits can be applied to offset alternative minimum tax: Allows all types of business credit to be used as an offset to AMT. Prior to 2010, business credits were only allowed to be used as offsets to income taxes if their tax was larger than the AMT tax.

Cell phones are includable business deduction: Previously, cell phones were considered personal property and disallowed as a business expense unless detailed usage records were kept. Now, they are treated as business property.

Limitation on penalties for tax reporting errors: Replaces the fixed dollar penalty applied to errors or failure to report certain transactions with a percentage penalty based on the reduction in taxes realized from the reporting error. This is to prevent some penalties from disproportionately effecting smaller businesses.

Referenced IRS Publications for More Information

Employer Identification Numbers (EIN) – Publication 1635, Understanding Your EIN

Accounting Periods and Methods – Publication 538

Self Employment Tax – Publication 533

Employer's tax Guide – Publication 15, Circular E

Tax Calendar for Filing and Paying Taxes, Publication 509

Cost of Goods Sold – Publication 538, Accounting Periods and Methods (See section in Inventories)

Business Expenses, Publication 535.

Section 2: Business Planning for Tax Efficiency

Although many small businesses don't reach a level of profitability until after a year or so, the failure to take the right steps early on to plan for taxes can prove to be very costly when the cash flow starts rolling in. Planning for taxes should not wait until the business is profitable, and even then, it should occur year round in order to take full advantage of the tax benefits available through the U.S. tax code.

Structuring Your Business for Taxes

Most businesses begin as a sole proprietorship or partnership because they are the easiest to create. Costs are usually a consideration for new businesses and these business forms require little or none. In both these forms, taxes are still tied to the individual rather than the business. Once in place, tax considerations can drive day-to-day decision-making, and tax planning can help keep your taxes to a minimum.

Incorporation

Once your business begins to generate profits, you may want to consider incorporating it under a C Corp or S Corp status. Both offer a greater level of tax efficiency, but they do so in different ways. They also are a more formal business structure requiring legal documentation, registration, formal operating policies, and more complex tax rules. The decision to incorporate should be made based on several factors besides tax consequences. Key considerations include:

- The amount of risk or liability exposure your business has
- The expectation of bigger and consistent profits
- An expectation that you will be obtaining public or private financing
- An expectation that you will be in the highest tax bracket

C-Corp Advantage

The primary tax advantage of a C-Corporation is that the owners only pay taxes on income in the form of salaries, bonuses and dividends that are actually received from the company. The owners can keep some of the profits inside the corporation where they are held as retained earnings and taxed at a lower corporate tax rate. Corporations only pay a 15% tax on the first $50,000 of retained earnings.

S-Corp Advantage

An S-Corp is a "pass through" tax entity, which means all profits and losses flow directly through to the shareholders. As a corporation, the shareholder can designate a specific amount of the profits to be paid as salary. In effect, this will enable the shareholder employees to control the amount of self employment taxes they pay. Considering that SE taxes can consume as much $15,000 (on $100,000 of income), by claiming only $50,000 of the profit as salary and the rest as dividends a shareholder employee can reduce his or her SE tax by half.

Tax Planning Moves to Make Now

Hire Your Family

It is perfectly legitimate for a business owner to hire family members as employees. Any compensation you pay them is deductible as a business expense. This is especially effective when you hire your children. For children under age 18, their wages are not taxed for Social Security, and for all of your children, you will have effectively shifted your income to the lower tax brackets of your children. It is important that you can document their legitimacy as employees in terms of their value to the business and the reasonableness of their compensation.

Additionally, you could set up a company tuition-reimbursement plan to pay your child's school cost. The plan can reimburse up to $5,250 in tuition per employee annually. Your child has to be an employee and over the age of 21, and cannot be claimed as a dependent.

Install a Section 105 HRA Plan

These plans are actually designed for small business owners who can hire their spouse. The plan allows the business to reimburse the spouse for medical expenses, which becomes a deductible expense for the business. If your family incurs large health and dental expenses, or you have high health insurance premiums, this plan can work to the advantage of both your family and your business. Additionally, your spouse can add you as a beneficiary to her plan, which means you should be able to deduct your medical costs as a business expense and get around the minimum floor requirement for personal itemized deductions.

Section 3: Doing Record Keeping that Works

The best tax planning in the world will be for naught if you have shoddy record keeping. In fact, it can cost you dearly in terms of penalties, missed tax savings, higher tax preparation fees, lost business opportunities and the inordinate amount of time it takes to correct poorly kept records. Conversely, an effective record keeping system can be a determining factor in the success of a business when a business owner understands how to use it to manage cash flow and maximize tax benefits.

Records Keeping Essentials

Keep personal and business records separate: Nothing can gum up your business record keeping more than mingling your personal expenses and records with those of your business. Open a separate business checking account and use a business debit or credit card for transactions. If you use your vehicle for both personal and business reasons, maintain a detailed log of its business use.

Use a T & E record keeping system that works for you: For many people, systematically logging records of client meetings, meal expenses, vehicle expenses, and travel expenses can be a difficult habit to develop or keep. Be sure to use what works for you, whether it is your current smart phone, a basic expense booklet, or a Filo-Fax, it needs to be able to record dates, places, names, business purposes and the expenses.

Keep supporting documents organized: The operation of a business can generate many different types of transaction paperwork. Expense receipts, receivables, asset purchases, employment records, tax forms, invoices, and statements to name a few. These are your supporting documents and are used to help you reconcile your books. Maintain separate files for each.

Keep your records daily: If you keep your records daily, then all you will see at the end the day is a mole-hill. Let it slip for a few days or a week and you will be looking at a mountain to climb, and that's where the errors and omissions start.

Get the Help You Need

Let's cut to the chase. No one likes to do record keeping, and, in fact, it is likely the last thing you thought about when you started your business. Business may be slow enough right now to allow you the time to do it on your own, but what happens when business picks up as expected? If you find yourself skipping your record keeping, either out of reluctance or a lack of time, you need to consider getting the help you need.

Virtual Bookkeeper

With the advent of the internet, and the growth in networked computer applications, it is easier and cheaper than ever to hire part-time help to manage your books. Virtual bookkeepers operate out of their home or as part of a company, and their services are offered on a pay for performance basis, or retainer. The average number of hours a small business would need to utilize a bookkeeper is about 20 hours per month.

Business Bookkeeping Software

If you insist on doing your own bookkeeping, you can save yourself a significant amount of time and money by investing in an accounting software program. Most brands are available for varying levels of need and sophistication. Even for the most basic needs, these programs include the essential journals and ledgers and are self-balancing as entries are made. Many programs will link to your business checking account so that your entries are downloaded to the software program. For the cost of a dinner out, you can have all of the bookkeeping power you need on your laptop.

Section 4: How to Calculate Estimate Taxes

Most small businesses that generate profits are required to make estimated tax payments. The IRS wants its taxes, and since you are not having your taxes withheld by an employer, it's coming directly to you for them. The surprise for many new business owners is that the estimated tax includes not only income taxes, but also self-employment taxes. And, to top it all off, the IRS wants you to be pretty darn accurate when you estimate your taxes. So, this is an aspect of your business you don't want to take lightly.

Who Makes Estimated Tax Payments?

Essentially any self-employed person or small business that expects to owe at least $1,000 more in taxes for the current year than in the prior year may be expected to make estimated tax payments. The determining factor is whether your current year's taxes are expected to approximate your previous year's taxes. If you expect that they will be less than 90% of the total taxes you paid last year, then you may not have to pay. If, however, you expect your current taxes to be at least 100% of your prior year's taxes, then you will definitely have to pay estimated taxes. If your income exceeded $150,000, then the threshold is increased to 110%.

How Much You Need to Pay

Because the determining factor for calculating estimated payments is based on a comparison of your prior year's taxes with your expected taxes for the current year, you need to carefully examine your prior year's tax return and then make some guesses as to any expected changes in it for the current year. For example, if you anticipate an increase in earnings, or a decrease in deductions, you could be facing a higher tax bill.

After accounting for all anticipated changes you can then estimate your next year's tax liability. The amount in excess of $1,000 would need to be paid as estimated payments throughout the year.

The IRS provides a worksheet (Form 1040-ES) that walks you through this process.

Paying Estimated Taxes

The more common method for paying estimated taxes is through quarterly installments. So, once you establish the amount of your total estimate taxes for the year, you simply divide it up into four equal payments.

For businesses that experience uneven revenue, an annualized method is available, in which you can make smaller, but more frequent installment payments. For this method, Form 2210, Underpayment of Estimated Tax, must be filed when you file your annual tax.

How to Lower Your Estimated Payments

This method will only work if you or your spouse works for an employer who withholds taxes. Simply by increasing your withholdings through the employer, you can reduce the amount of your estimated tax payments. The withheld taxes are taken into account when you calculate your total taxes paid in the prior year. It would be important to make sure that the additional withholding amount raises your total tax withholding for the year so that it is at least 90% of the amount you expect to owe, less $1,000, or so that it is at least 100% of the total taxes you paid last year, less $1,000, whichever is less.

Section 5: Small Business Capital Gains and Losses

Most small business owners are well versed on the tax implications of business income and deductions. But, for those businesses that buy, own and sell business assets, the rules can become a bit more involved. Capital gains and losses are treated similarly for businesses as they are for individuals, but differences exist depending on the reporting requirements of the particular type of business and its tax structure.

What are Business Capital Gains?

A capital gain is a form of income that results from the sale of an asset owned by a business, or the liquidation of an investment. A business that owns equipment or real estate is going to incur a capital gain or loss upon its sale. Products that are sold by a business for purposes of generating profits are not considered capital assets, and the revenue from their sale is considered income from sales.

As with individuals, the length of the holding periods of assets by a business will determine the capital gains tax rate that is applied. A short-term holding period is one year or less, in which gains are taxed at the ordinary income tax rate, while a long-term holding period is beyond twelve months, after which the gains are taxed at the capital gains tax rates. Currently the capital tax rate is 15% (0% for lower income individuals), but it is scheduled to increase to 20% beginning in 2012.

Capital Gain Treatment in Different Business Structures

Essentially, in those business forms that are considered to be "pass-through" tax entities, the capital gain or loss incurred from the sale of a business asset flows through to the business owner, partners or shareholder, so the actual tax that is applied is according to individual tax rules. For the most part, owners of these businesses will incur a capital gains tax rate of 15%.

Businesses that are incorporated and subject to corporate income tax rates are treated as separate tax entities. Therefore, any capital gains are realized by the business and taxed at its corporate tax rate. While the capital gains tax rate is the same for corporations as it is with individuals, the business reports the capital gains and pays the tax.

Determining Capital Gains and Losses

Upon the sale of an asset, the cost basis of the asset is subtracted from its selling price to determine the capital gain or loss. The cost basis includes the original outlay minus any depreciation. The gain or loss is then reported on Schedule D. If the asset was held for a year or less, it is reported as a short term gain or loss. If the holding period was more than a year, it is reported as a long term capital gain. Short term and long term gains and losses are reported separately and taxed at their respective rates.

Section 6: Financing Options and Their Tax Implications

Obtaining financing for a small business is a challenge for business owners. Either they are too new to qualify for bank loans, too small to attract investors, or they have already tapped out their family, friends, and their personal credit cards. The prospects for obtaining financing are not always going to be bleak, and opportunities for debt financing will emerge. When they do, it is important to choose the right kind of financing to best suit your situation.

Credit Card Financing

The tales of companies like Google starting with nothing more than credit card financing are legendary, but rare. Still, credit cards are the only source of funds for many new businesses. The obvious downside is their high interest costs, and, for a new business, the payments can eat into operating costs. Credit card financing can work if it is used effectively and for short term purposes.

Ideally, the use of credit cards should be limited to purchases of materials or products that can be immediately converted to revenue. For instance, if you receive an order for a service or goods from a customer, the materials or inventory you'll need to fulfill the order can be charged to your credit card in anticipation of generating the revenue that will cover the charge before you incur excessive finance charges. Of course, you can build the added cost of interest into your pricing, but if the turnaround time is too long, you will lose your profit. If you have to, you can pay off one credit card charge with another credit card in order to control the finance charges.

It is never wise to use your credit cards to finance long term purchases such as equipment unless you expect to be able to cover the cost within a relatively short period of time.

Tax Implications: Financing charges incurred from credit card use is tax deductible if it can be shown that the charges were used for business purposes. If your business is structured as a pass-through entity, such as a sole proprietorship, partnership or S Corp, these deduction flow through to your personal tax return (Schedule C). It is vital that you maintain detailed records of all business purchases with supporting documents.

Bank Loans

It's not impossible to obtain bank financing, but you need to be able to present a strong case to the lender. That means having some credit history for your business, a strong business plan, short-term prospects for profitability, good current cash flow, a specific business purpose for the loan, a co-signer, and personal collateral. Short of any of that, you probably shouldn't try. If you do qualify, your bank will require regular accounting of the use of the funds as well as well as updated cash flow statements.

Most banks will require your spouse to be a co-signer on the loan, which means that both your separate property and your jointly-held property can be subject to liens by the bank in the event of default. Additionally, if your spouse has a job, his or her earnings can be garnished following a judgment of default.

Tax Implications: Interest expenses from business bank loans are tax deductible.

Friends or Family

A common source of financing is through friends or family. It is important that loans from these sources be formalized through a promissory note. This keeps your transaction on a business level, and it legitimatizes the loan in the eyes of the IRS. The interest rate must be reasonably equivalent to commercial rates for the IRS to consider it a legitimate business loan.

Tax Implications: If the loan meets IRS guidelines, the interest charged is tax deductible.

Section 7: Best Retirement Plan Options for Business Owners

Providing employee benefits such as retirement plans and health insurance is important for small businesses, as much for the ability to recruit and retain quality employees as for the financial security of the business owners. Initially, small businesses may be reluctant to offer benefits due to their administrative burden as well as their perceived costs. And, while it is true that some types of plans can increase administrative and business costs, by choosing the right kind of plan, the benefits ultimately outweigh the costs.

Whether you are the sole employee or you employ several people, choosing the right retirement plan is critical to ensure that you are providing the optimum level of benefits while controlling your costs. Additionally, as a business owner, it is important to capture every tax advantage available to you.

Best Retirement Plan Options

Solo 401(k)

If you have no or few employees, and your goal is to defer as much as your income as possible, the solo 401(k) may be your best option. This plan is, in essence, the small business version of the popular 401(k) used by larger companies. Compared with other small business options, these plans allow for higher retirement savings contributions, currently $16,500 per year ($22,000 if you are age 50 or older (Contribution limits for 2011)).

Additionally, while other retirement plan options, such as the SEP IRA, allow for contributions up to 20% of the owners net business profit up to $49,000, solo 401(k) plans allow for 100% of your income up to $16,500, plus 20% of net profit up to $49,000 ($54,000 for ages 50 and older).

If you have employees, they can elect to participate under the same contribution rules. Most employers provide a match contribution up to 3% of the employee's contribution, which is tax deductible for the employer.

These plans can be set up through any number of mutual funds or discount brokerage firms which charge a fee for administrating the plans. When the plan's total assets reaches a certain level the employer is required to file reports each year that can increase administrative and accounting costs. Typically a plan administrator can handle this task.

SEP IRA

If you don't think you will be able to defer anywhere near the maximum amount of income each year, a SEP IRA may be a better option because they are the easiest and least costly to administer. A business owner can contribute up to 20% of net profits to the plan up to $49,000.*

With a SEP IRA, the employer makes all of the contributions on behalf of the employees. However, they are not mandatory, so if no profits are generated for the year, no contributions have to be made. Another advantage is that although all contributions are to be made by the employer, they are not mandatory, so the employer can manage its contributions around the company's profitability.

SIMPLE IRA

If you have a dozen or more employees and are more concerned with covering everyone with a retirement benefit, SIMPLE IRA may be your best option. It's simple to set up and administer and is the best option for controlling your overall outlay. Employees are responsible for their own contributions, which are deducted from their salary. The contribution limit is only $11,500 (Contribution limits for 2011), but an employer can add matching contributions of 3% of the employee's contributions.

Section 8: Getting the Most from Your Business Deductions (While Staying Out of Trouble)

One of the biggest advantages of operating your own business is that nearly every activity you perform that incurs an expense is tax deductible. That's the good news. The bad news is that, if you keep poor records, and you are not paying attention on a daily basis to the tax implications of your business activities, you are likely to miss out on some valuable deductions, and worse, irritate the IRS agent during your tax audit.

Which Business Expenses are Deductible?

The easiest way to ensure that you are getting the most from your business deductions is to organize your activities and record keeping system around your deductible business expenses. Generally, expenses are deductible if they are considered to be "ordinary" and "necessary" in the operation of your business. The following is a list of deductible expenses common to most businesses:

- Advertising: Expenses associated with promoting and marketing your business such as newspaper and television ads. Business cards are an advertising expense.
- Business Development Fees: Fees paid to non-employees for referrals and business development.
- Contract Labor: Payments made for any out-sourced activities such as for a virtual bookkeeper
- Insurance: Premiums paid for any business-related insurance such as liability or business property insurance. Homeowner and vehicle insurance may be deductible to the extent your house and car are used for business purposes.
- Interest Expense: Mortgage interest on business property and any interest expense incurred through business debt including credit card finance charges, and installment loan interest.
- Office Expenses: Purchases of supplies, postage, books, and reference materials used exclusively in your business are all deductible.
- Supplies: Items used in the conduct of your business, such as maintenance, cleaning supplies, packaging materials.
- Legal and Professional Fees: Fees paid for the services of an attorney, accountant, a financial

planner, or tax preparer are deductible if the services are necessary for the business.

- Rent or Lease: Rent payments for the use of business property are deductible.
- Licenses: If your business requires a license of any kind, the costs associated with acquiring and maintaining it are deductible.
- Taxes: Taxes incurred as a result of the operation of your business are generally deductible. These include property taxes, state or local income taxes, and retail sales taxes. All taxes associated with payroll, such as Social Security, Medicare, FUTA, and state unemployment tax.
- Wages: Any form of compensation paid to an employee is a deductible expense, including employee benefits such as health plan and retirement plan contributions.
- Health Insurance Premiums: Generally, health insurance premiums are deductible to the extent that you have income.
- Travel: An expense incurred by you or an employee while away from home for business purposes are tax deductible, including transportation, car rental, baggage shipping, and lodging.
- Meals and Entertainment: Any activity performed with a client considered to be ordinary and necessary for a clear business

purpose, such as entertainment, dining, or recreation (golf outing). The deduction for these expenses is limited to 50%. Business gifts are also deductible up to one deduction per year, per customer of $25.

- Education Expenses: The cost of tuition and books for education related to your current trade or business can be deducted if they meet strict guidelines.

- Bad Debt: If a receivable was recorded as part of gross revenue, it may be deducted if it is ultimately deemed to be uncollectable. Cash method accounting does not allow for bad debt deductions.

- Start-up Costs: Under the American Jobs Creation Act, expenses associated with the start-up of a business may be deductible. New business owners are allowed to deduct up to $5,000 for start-up costs and another $5,000 for organizational expenses that are incurred in the first year of the business. Expenses that are not incurred in the first year may be amortized over 15 years.

- Vehicle Expenses: Generally all of the expenses incurred while operating a vehicle for business purposes are deductible. If you or an employee uses a personal car for business purposes, the portion of expenses actually incurred while using it for business are deductible. You may choose between two methods for determining vehicle expenses:

- Actual expenses – The actual operating costs of the vehicle are reported, including maintenance, fuel, registration, storage, insurance, and depreciation (if you personally own the vehicle).

- Standard mileage – If you own or lease your vehicle, you can apply the standard mileage rate (the 2010 rate is $.51 per mile) to the miles driven for business purposes. You can use this method if it has been applied since the vehicle was placed in the service of your business. Fees for parking, tolls, finance charges and taxes (applicable to the business use of the vehicle) may be added to the standard mileage calculation.

- Depreciation: Property acquired for use in your business is not fully deductible in the year it is purchased. Instead, the cost is allocated, or depreciated over multiple tax years. Business property such as furniture, buildings, computer equipment is included as depreciable assets. Section 179 of the tax code allows for a certain portion of the property expense to be deducted in the first year as a depreciation allowance. The allowance is capped in 2011 at $500,000, but that is expected to drop to $125,000 in 2012.

Business Use of Your Home

If you use your home or a part of it exclusively for business, you may be able to deduct a proportionate amount of your home's expenses, such as mortgage interest, utilities, repairs, and insurance on your Schedule C (Form 8829, Expenses for Business Use of Your Home is used to calculate expenses). You must be able to meet some strict requirements in order to establish that your home is your principle place of business.

Managing Your Deductions

Remember, all of your business expenses have to be ordinary and necessary to the operation of your business. Each expense must be logged and a supporting document, such as a receipt or cancelled check must be on file and ready to present to the IRS. On any given day, you are likely to generate a dozen or more deductions in the course of conducting regular business activities, so it is easy for some to slip through the cracks, so it is vitally important to have a sound record keeping system in place in order to get the most from your deductions and avoid any problems.

Section 9: Online Resources and Tax Help for Small Businesses

Between record keeping, estimate payments, managing deductions, making retirement plan contributions, and making year-end tax planning decisions, business owners are in constant tax planning and preparation mode, 365 days a year. Hopefully, all was not put off until tax filing time, but even if it were, there are a number of online resources that can help both planners and procrastinators understand, organize, manage, prepare and file their taxes.

Year-Round Help

Document Management

When tax preparation tends to break down it is usually due to poor record keeping. Lost receipts, misfiled documents, and general chaos in the organization of documents is endemic among small businesses. As a result, valuable deductions are missed, or shot down in an audit due to a lack of supporting documentation.

Technology has made it much easier to manage, and even reduce your paperwork and filing needs. Online resources such as Shoeboxed.com provide digitizing services for your business receipts and other financial documents. Additionally, it can unlock all of the important data from your documents and help you organize it into spreadsheets or other accounting tools such as Quicken. By simply scanning the day's receipts onto your computer, Shoeboxed.com takes over as your virtual record keeping assistant. You can also use it to scan and organize contact information from business cards.

Forum Participation

Many times the best source for answers to your questions or solving problems is by talking with other business owners. At the very least it is sometimes nice to know that you are not alone in your problems and misery. Tapping into active online forums such as Intuit Community (**http://community.intuit.com/**), gives you 24/7 access to a nationwide community of business owners and small business experts posing and solving tax problems. It is worthwhile to schedule twenty minutes a week to pipe into these types of forums as you will be learning about the hottest and latest tax issues facing business owners.

Sites like H&R Block Get it Right (**http://getitright.hrblock.com/**) allow you to ask a tax-related question and receive a response from a CPA or tax expert. Or, you can go right to the source and have access to a wide range of resources at your fingertips through the Small Business and Self-Employed Tax Center at the IRS (**http://www.irs.gov/businesses/small/index.html**).

Tax Preparation and Filing in the Cloud

More and more people are gravitating towards online or software-based tax preparation programs, many of which are free or relatively inexpensive. Unfortunately, most of these programs aren't sufficiently equipped to handle the tax issues for a small business, especially when specific business tax forms are required.

For a small investment, some of these programs can be upgraded to accommodate most small business needs, and the better ones will provide step-by-step guidance as well as online support for preparing your tax forms. If you are stuck on an issue, you can access their communities of experts to answer your questions fairly quickly.

TurboTax for Small Business (**http://turbotax.intuit.com/small-business-taxes/**), is probably the most widely used, and they offer various versions depending on whether you are a sole proprietor (Home & Business), a C-Corp, S-Corp or Partnership (Business). H&R Block Tax (**http://www.hrblock.com/tax-software/index.html**), also offers two versions based on the structure of your business. Both offer free IRS e-filing as part of their fees.

Alternatively, for those daring enough to complete their business tax forms on their own, the IRS offers its own online resource, IRS e-file for Small Business and Self-Employed Taxpayers (**http://www.irs.gov/efile/article/0,,id=118520,00.html**), where you have access to all of the forms you need, free e-filing, and documented help guides.

Of course, it is always recommended that you have your competed returns reviewed by a CPA or small business tax expert before filing. While you incur an added expense for professional services, the amount of fees you'll pay will be substantially less than if you simply have them do all of the work from the beginning. And remember, professional tax preparation fees are deductible.

Section 10: Year-End Tax Planning for Business Owners

As has been emphasized throughout this guide, tax planning for small business owners is a year-round endeavor. For many small businesses, it is not until they approach the end of the year that they have a better understanding of their business' financial situation as it relates to profits, cash flow anticipation, expense allotments, and their tax consequences. Taking the opportunity to review the business' books in order to assess possible year-end tax savings strategies is the biggest opportunity an owner has to save on taxes in the current year while looking a year ahead for more tax savings.

How to Achieve Year-End Tax Savings

For any of these year-end tax saving strategies, your business's tax structure and accounting method should be considered. Also, before taking any tax-saving action this year, it is important to consider its impact on your tax situation in the coming year.

Defer year-end income: If you are a sole proprietor, S Corp or partnership using the cash method of accounting, any receivables you can defer into the next tax year will save taxes this year. This method may not make sense if you anticipate that your income tax rate will rise substantially in the coming year.

Accelerate expenses: Looking ahead, if you anticipate purchasing supplies, you can accelerate the deduction into the current year by making the purchases now. The same for any accounts payable such as utilities, rent or insurance for your business – make your January payments in December.

Maximize your Section 179 deduction: If you are planning any major equipment purchases, such as a new computer, a company car, or machinery, accelerate the purchase into the current year to take full advantage of the Section 179 depreciation allowance that allows for accelerated depreciation and a deduction of the full purchase price in the current year.

Write down your inventory: If you have inventory that is just sitting on the shelves, it is probably costing you more than if you just wrote it off. You have to offer the inventory for sale first, and if it doesn't move, you can remove it from the shelves and write-off its fair market value.

Donate it to charity: A better option for your inventory may be to donate it to charity. A deduction for the fair market value can be taken which can result in more cash flow through tax savings than if the item were sold at a salvage price or simply junked.

Set up a retirement plan: If you haven't done so, establish a retirement plan (see section 7 The Best Retirement Plan Options for Business Owners). Be sure to review the contribution timing requirements, as some plans require contributions to be made by October.

Review your business structure: Changing the structure of your business is a major decision that can have long term implications in the area of taxes, profits, your personal finances, and the growth potential of you business, so it should only be done with the guidance of a business planning expert. At some point, business owners might be able to benefit by changing their structure from a sole proprietorship to an S Corp, or even a C Corp. This change should only be considered if you anticipate significant increases in profits and you plan to obtain public or private financing.

www.ingramcontent.com/pod-product-compliance
Lightning Source LLC
Chambersburg PA
CBHW071626170526
45166CB00003B/1211